From Our Hearts to Yours,

A THINKING *of* OTHERS BOOK

Book Four: Encouraging Others

Cody's Castle

Written by
Gary Bower

Illustrated by
Jan Bower

Storybook Meadow
Traverse City, Michigan

ACKNOWLEDGMENTS

I want to thank my family for helping me to appreciate the importance of encouraging words. The idea for this story came from actually watching my kids help each other deal with their fears and insecurities. My thanks also goes to the friends and family members who have so graciously used their words to build me up.

- *Gary Bower*

Once again, I'm grateful for all the wonderful children who posed (actually *played*) and allowed me to photograph them to be painted later. Specifically, thank you Clark Morgan (Cody), Angel Bower (Emily), Justin Kraft (Wyatt), Michaela Jamison (Sarah), Carmen Jamison (Grace), and Rachel Jamison (Mom). I was blessed with beautiful subjects on a beautiful Michigan day on the Sleeping Bear Dunes National Lakeshore on Lake Michigan.

- *Jan Bower*

Cody's Castle

Published by Storybook Meadow Publishing
7700 Timbers Trail, Traverse City, MI 49684

Library of Congress Control Number: 2004091955

ISBN 0-9704621-3-1

Printed and bound in Canada

To Austin,
who is careful to make sure that his wit doesn't wound.

Cody rocked his horse so wildly that his hat almost flew off. "*Yee-haw!*" he yelled. "I'm storming the castle!"

"Cowboys don't storm castles, knights do," his sister, Sarah, corrected him. "And knights don't say 'yee-haw.'"

Cody kept on storming the castle anyway.

"Somebody needs to burn some energy," said Mom. "Who wants to go to the beach?"

Cody tumbled off the horse even before he stopped it. "I do!"

"Me, too!" Sarah chimed in, scampering up the stairs to change.

"Beach!" said two-year-old Grace.

Minutes later, Mom buckled Grace into her car seat as Sarah fastened her seatbelt in the back seat.

Mom paused to make sure she wasn't forgetting anything. "I guess we're ready," she said.

"Not yet," hollered Cody as he disappeared around the corner of the house. He returned with a yellow pail and a blue shovel.

"Now we're ready!"

On their way to the beach, they stopped to pick up Sarah's friend, Emily, who was sitting in her yard with her kitten.

"I have to go now, Buttercup," she said, stroking its soft neck. "Don't get into any mischief."

Buttercup looked at her with sad eyes.

“Poor Buttercup,” said Emily as she climbed into the car. “She wanted to come.”

“Cats don’t like the water, anyway,” Cody said.

“I don’t either,” Emily replied. “I just like playing in the sand.”

That puzzled Cody. He couldn’t understand why anyone wouldn’t like the water.

All the way to the beach the girls giggled at the funny things Cody said, and the more they giggled, the funnier he tried to be.

"You're all silly," said Mom, parking the car. "We're here…finally. Everyone carry something."

The fresh smell of the lake pulled Cody toward it like a fish on a line. He spotted an umbrella that he recognized.

"Wyatt's here!"

"His mother said they'd meet us here," Mom explained.

Cody sped away to join his friend.

"Last one in is a sea turtle!"

The boys' feet kicked up a spray as they struck the shoreline. Slower and slower Cody's legs moved as the water reached his knees, then his waist. *Sploosh!* He plunged in head first.

Wyatt disappeared beneath the water's surface, too. The boys came up at the same time, wiping their faces and laughing.

"Gotcha!" Wyatt shouted, splashing Cody.

"Oh yeah?" Cody answered, flailing his arms wildly.

Gallons of water showered in all directions until the boys had to stop to catch their breath.

"The girls!" panted Cody. "Let's get 'em!"

"Yeah!" Wyatt agreed.

Sarah and Emily stood watching from the beach as the boys made their way toward them.

"Aren't you coming in?" Cody asked.

Sarah was cautious. "Promise not to splash?"

The boys looked at each other.

"Sure," said Cody.

Wyatt smirked.

Cautiously, Sarah ventured out to her ankles, but Emily didn't budge. She just stared at the water, digging her toes into the sand.

"C'mon," said Wyatt, taking her by the arm.

Emily pulled away. "I don't want to."

"She's scared," said Cody.

"Of what?" Wyatt replied. "Sharks?"

Cody snickered.

Emily scowled at them. "Sharks live in the ocean. This is a lake," she said sharply.

"Swimming's easy," Wyatt boasted. "I can swim like a fish!"

"Emily's not a fish," Cody said. "She's more like a kitten. She only likes the sand."

Both boys snickered.

Emily's lip quivered slightly. "It's not funny," she mumbled, walking away.

Sarah glared at the boys.

"We were just kidding," said Cody.

"You shouldn't make fun of people," Sarah shot back. Then she ran to catch up to her friend.

The boys decided to play in the sand. Wyatt dug a hole so deep that water seeped in from the bottom.

"In a minute, you'll be taller than me," he told Cody. Then he hopped down into the hole and began to fill the hole around him with sand.

Cody went to work on a sand castle. For the next half hour, he worked intently along the shore. He dug and he dumped. He poured and he piled. He scooped and he sculpted. Finally, his castle was finished.

"Look, Mom!" he said proudly. "I built the biggest castle on the whole beach!"

"You certainly did," Mom replied. "That's quite a castle."

Just then, a white, foamy wave reached out and washed away part of the castle.

"Uh-oh!" said Cody. He hurried to pack sand around the the base of the castle, but immediately another wave swept even more sand away. He worked faster and faster.

Frustrated, he turned to Mom, who sat with Grace on a beach towel.

"I can't do it," he groaned.

Suddenly, the side of the castle closest to the shore collapsed. Cody watched helplessly as huge chunks of his castle slid into the lake.

"Maybe you should try building a new castle a little farther from the water," Mom suggested.

Cody picked up his pail and shovel and headed for drier ground.

"Ow! Ooo! Ow!" The sand was getting hot. He chose a new spot to build, burrowing his feet deep into the sand to cool them.

Cody filled his pail with sand and quickly tipped it over to make a sand tower. *Thump*. But when he lifted the pail, the sand fell, too dry to hold its shape.

"This isn't working," he complained.

"It will if you add a little water," said Mom.

"That's what tore down my first castle," Cody grumbled.

"Maybe you should just try it."

Cody ran back to the shore with his bucket. Soon, he had a new castle even bigger than the last one. Mom and Grace came over to see it.

"Wow. Very nice," Mom praised him.

"Vee-wee nice," echoed Grace.

Cody felt proud as they admired his work. Then a thought popped into his head.

"Isn't it weird, Mom? Water ruined my first castle, but helped me build this one."

Mom raised her eyebrows. "Interesting," she said. "You know, words are like that, too."

"Huh?"

Mom bent down so their eyes could meet.

"Words can build people up or tear them down."

She gazed at the beach. Cody turned his head that direction. There was Emily, playing with Sarah along the shore.

"Why doesn't Emily like the water, anyway?" Cody asked.

"There are lots of reasons people are afraid of things," Mom replied, "but instead of teasing Emily, maybe you should try encouraging her."

Cody squirmed. "I'm not very good at that."

Mom's response was gentle. "You could be. Maybe you should try."

Hmm, thought Cody, *maybe*.

Minutes later, Cody and Wyatt were ready to go back into the water. Emily and Sarah were burying each other's feet in the sand.

"Sorry for teasing you," Cody said meekly.

"Me, too," said Wyatt. "But you don't need to be scared of the water, Emily. It's really fun!"

"Everybody's afraid of something," Sarah defended her friend.

Cody thought for a moment. "Actually, I don't like holding cats," he admitted sheepishly.

Emily's eyes widened in surprise. "You don't? But they're so soft and cuddly!"

"They always scratch me," said Cody.

"Maybe you don't hold them right," Emily said.

"Maybe." Cody looked at the water. "Come here," he said, taking her hand. "I promise not to splash."

Emily resisted for just a second, then cautiously took a few steps into the water. "Not too fast...not too fast!" she said.

"The water's really warm," said Cody. "And isn't the bottom sandy?"

"Yeah," Emily agreed.

Cody led her gently. They waded out until the water nearly reached Emily's waist.

"That's deep enough," she said nervously.

"You're doing great," Cody encouraged her. "Wanna get your face wet?"

"No!" Emily answered abruptly.

"Okay," said Cody, "you don't have to. But if you ever decide that you want to, all you have to do is hold your breath, like this." Cody dunked his head and brought it back up.

Emily stared down at the water.

"Maybe you should try it," Cody suggested.

Emily hesitated. Then she squeezed her eyes shut, took a big breath and held her nose. As she lowered her head, her bangs dangled in the water. Slowly, her face, then her ears, and finally her entire head went under. She jerked her head up quickly.

"You did it!" Cody shouted as Sarah and Wyatt cheered.

"I did it!" Emily beamed.

All the rest of that fun afternoon, Cody and the others watched Emily grow braver and braver. Once she even snuck up behind Cody.

"Oh, *Co-dy!*" she called sweetly.

Cody turned just as a spray of water hit him in the face. He paused for a moment – then everything went wild!

Cody found it hard to believe that Emily had ever been scared at all.

As the afternoon drew to a close, Mom made arrangements with Wyatt's mother for him to spend the night. Five tired children gathered toys and towels.

"It's been a pleasant day," Mom said with a sigh.

"What was the best part?" asked Sarah.

"The sunshine," Mom answered.

"Building sand castles," said Cody.

"Swimming," said Wyatt.

"Splashing!" shouted Emily.

Sarah smiled at her friend. "You looked like you were having lots of fun."

"I was!"

As they walked past Cody's castle, everyone stopped to admire it one last time.

Mom stooped to talk in Cody's ear. "I think a lot of building up took place today," she said softly. "I'm proud of you." And she planted a kiss on his cheek.

Cody rubbed his ear. "That tickles!" he giggled.

"Looky!" squealed Grace.

A little ice cream shop sat beside the parking lot, right where hot, hungry children would be sure to see it.

"Oh boy!" said Cody. "Could we?"

"It's too close to dinnertime," Mom objected. "We can't eat ice cream now without spoiling our appetites."

A mischievous grin spread across Cody's face. "Maybe we should try," he suggested.

"Hmm…" said Mom,

SHAKES & MALTS

"...maybe we should."

*Let everything you say be good and helpful,
so that your words will be an encouragement
to those who hear them."*

Ephesians 4:29

Can you remember?

What was the name of Emily's kitten?

What did Cody like to make people do?

Of what was Emily afraid? Was Cody afraid of anything?

What did Cody's mother encourage him to try?
What did Cody encourage Emily to try?
What did Cody encourage his mother to try?

Why weren't there any sharks at that beach?

What do you think?

How are words like water?

Why was Emily willing to go into the water
at the end, but not at the beginning?

What's the right way to make people laugh?
What's the wrong way?

What kinds of words build people up?
What kinds of words tear people down?

When has someone encouraged you?
Who do you know that needs to be encouraged?

A Word from the Author
to
Parents & Teachers

Once one of my children sliced up some vegetables for a salad, but failed to use a cutting board. Jan and I were less than thrilled to see the scratches that were made on our formica countertop. The scratches were unintentional, of course; the goal was only to make a tasty salad. Nevertheless, the marks were there to stay.

In ***Cody's Castle***, Cody made the same careless mistake. He was simply trying to create a few laughs, oblivious to the fact that his "cutting up" was hurting someone else.

Making others laugh is a gift and an art. Some people skillfully use their humor to brighten up a room, and their quick wit can keep a conversation interesting and moving along. Society needs comedians!

The flip side, unfortunately, is that witty people often speak before they think. Like a truck with no brakes, they get on a roll, gaining momentum rapidly. Soon they're speeding downhill, capable of causing serious injury.

While most funny people aren't mean-spirited, many of them don't stop to consider the power their words have. That's certainly been true in my case. For a long time, I sought the laugh without giving much thought to the scar that might linger. I'm thankful for a wife who patiently instilled a new perspective in me over the years.

Cody's Castle has a clear lesson: not only don't words have to tear down and ridicule, *they also can be used to build up and encourage.* Encouragement is an art that can be learned. Just as a comedian works hard to polish his act, wanting his words and presentation to be effective at producing a laugh, an encourager can also hone his skills. By using just the right words in just the right way, a person can produce courage, hope, faith, peace, love, and many other positive responses.

It's easy to develop the bad habit of letting hurtful remarks roll off our tongues. And, of course, old habits are hard to change.

But maybe we should try.